Haiku Gold

a haiku for each autumn day

P.J. REED

Lost Tower Publications

first published in 2021
Reedited in 2025
by Lost Tower Publications

P.J. Reed asserts her copyright over this collection of her work.
P.J. Reed is identified as the author of this work in accordance with
Section 77 of the Copyright, Designs and Patents Act 1988.

This book is sold subject to the condition that it shall not, by way
of trade or otherwise, be lent, hired out or otherwise circulated
without the publisher's prior consent in any form or cover than that
in which it is published.

ISBN: 9780957071186

Haiku Gold

also by P.J. Reed

HAIKU NATION

The Haiku Seasons Collection

HAIKU YELLOW
HAIKU SUN
HAIKU GOLD
HAIKU ICE

Simply Senryu

PANDEMICA

Haiku Gold

Foreword

Autumn is the perfect pause between extremes.

The fire of summer has passed, and the cold of winter waits just beyond the horizon. The temperature sits gently on the skin, and all you need for wandering is a jumper or a raincoat. It is the season of colour, bold hues of gold, red, and brown. Each fallen leaf holds a slightly different shade, each one its own farewell.

Haiku Gold is a memory of Devon autumns; a gallery of moments caught in miniature.

This is the third book in my seasonal haiku collections, exploring how the changing year shapes the woods, fields, hedgerows, plants, and animals of the Devon countryside.

Haiku are brief, but never empty. They hold entire worlds inside them. A memory caught before it fades. A season resting in the palm of your hand. The hush of a feeling too delicate for ordinary words.

Inside this book you will find one haiku for every day of autumn, from September 22 to December 21, following the astronomical calendar, though the dates vary slightly every year.

I told one reader that I was writing a collection of autumn poetry, and she told me quite frankly that she would never read a poetry book about autumn. Apparently, reading a hundred-plus poems about 'falling golden leaves forming a crunchy carpet' was not her idea of a good time!

Therefore, in this collection I have tried to be very careful and leave the 'falling golden leaf' descriptions to a minimum!

So, what is special about autumn?

The season of autumn has its own scent.

The first rain on sun-baked soil softens the ground underfoot. Fallen leaves decay into the rich, waiting earth. Ripe apples drop from heavy branches, scenting the grass with cidery sweetness. The air fills with smoke from evening fires, Halloween bonfires, and fireworks bursting into the night.

It is a season of abundance.

Hedgerows brim with blackberries that ripen from green to crimson to deep black. Blackthorn branches gleam with blue sloes ready for preserves. In the fields, pumpkins swell like tethered orange balloons along their curling vines.

It is the season of mini miracles.

Most of these haiku were written while wandering the countryside with Rupert, my rescue hound.

The September 23 haiku was written after visiting Saunton Sands, a wild North Devon beach, on an overcast day on my eldest daughter's birthday. The stormy sea mirrored the grey sky. A few surfers dared the waves, while dog walkers trudged along the shore. Then the storm ended, and the tide withdrew, leaving behind a trail of small wonders. One of these became the haiku for that day.

Another of my favourite walks follows an old canal that winds through the fields and woodland. Moorhens and mallards weave between the reeds and tall bulrushes. Every time you pause near the edge, an eager armada of ducks appears as if summoned. The *haiku* from October 11 captures one such ambush.

One windy afternoon, while walking my dog, I noticed a single stubborn leaf trembling on an otherwise bare branch. I paused and wondered if trees mourn their fallen leaves, if they feel the slow quieting of their own beauty. That moment became the haiku of November 12.

I have always loved the wild visitors to my garden, especially the woodpigeons who visit each morning. Once, nine gathered on the lawn, heads down in perfect unison. Another morning, I woke to find the holly tree stripped of its ruby berries, while the same plump pigeons watched from the fence, looking very pleased with themselves. That scene became the haiku of November 13.

Autumn is not about endings but about remembering to see. It reminds us to slow down, to notice what slips past us, to hold still long enough to explore the beauty of nature in transition.

The *haiku* are designed to be read slowly, greeting every morning with a single image or ending the evening with a quiet moment of reflection. Some readers treat them as meditations, others as affirmations, and some simply enjoy them as tiny pockets of beauty.

Although shaped by Devon's landscape, *Haiku Gold* carries the spirit of traditional Japanese haiku. It invites you to look closely, to love the small and the ordinary, and to find poetry hidden in the quiet corners of daily life.

Above all, *Haiku Gold* is a celebration of autumn, my favourite season. A time touched with magic, when the greens of summer give way to golds, reds, and browns. When every step falls onto a carpet of crisp colour.

Autumn has its own language of scent. The first rain on sun-baked soil softens the ground underfoot. Fallen leaves decay into the rich, waiting earth. Ripe apples drop from heavy branches, scenting the grass with sweetness. The air fills with smoke from evening fires, from Halloween bonfires and fireworks bright against the night.

It is also a season of abundance. Hedgerows brim with blackberries that ripen from green to crimson to deep black. Blackthorn branches gleam with blue sloes ready for preserves. In the fields, pumpkins swell like tethered orange balloons along their curling vines.

The September 23 *haiku* was written after visiting Saunton Sands, a wild North Devon beach, on an overcast day for my eldest daughter's birthday. The sea mirrored the grey sky, restless beneath clouds. Only a few surfers floated in the distance, and dog walkers traced the shore while the tide withdrew, leaving behind a trail of small wonders. One of these became the haiku for that day.

Another of my favourite walks follows the old canal that winds through the fields and woodland. Moorhens and mallards weave between the reeds, and the water glints through tall bulrushes. But wildness here has its humour too. Every time you pause near the edge, an eager armada of ducks appears as if summoned. The haiku from October 11 captures one such ambush.

One windy afternoon, while walking my dog, I noticed a single stubborn leaf trembling on an otherwise bare branch. I wondered if trees mourn their fallen leaves, if they feel the slow quieting of their own beauty. That moment became the *haiku* of November 12.

I have always loved the rhythm of our garden, especially the woodpigeons who visit each morning. Once, nine gathered on the lawn, heads down in perfect unison. Another morning, I woke to find the holly tree stripped of its ruby berries, while the same plump pigeons watched from the fence, looking very pleased with themselves. That scene became the *haiku* of November 13.

Above all, autumn is about remembering to see. It reminds us to slow down, to notice what slips past us, to hold still long enough to explore the beauty of nature in transition.

I hope these poems will give you a moment of quiet wonder, a wry eyebrow raise, or even a happy smile!

'*This collection is more than seasonal poetry; it's a heartfelt conversation between the poet and the reader. P.J. Reed's Haiku Gold evokes the crispness of fall air and the quiet charm of country life with remarkable elegance. The addition of behind-the-scenes stories offers a deeper connection, making each poem feel like a shared memory. It's the perfect companion for chilly days, warming you from the inside out with its golden imagery and authentic voice.*' T.

'*Haiku Gold by P. J. Reed is a quiet, beautifully observed journey through the Devon countryside as it slips from summer into autumn. Each haiku captures small, fleeting moments: mist rising over fields, leaves turning, the hush before rain with a calm precision that feels both grounded and tender. Reed's choice to include brief notes about how certain haiku came to life adds warmth and personality, giving the collection an almost diary-like intimacy. The imagery is rich and sensory, evoking the scent of wet leaves and the soft light of fading days. A perfect read for anyone who loves nature writing, haiku, or simply wants to pause and breathe in autumn's calm.*' A.A.

'*This is a wonderful collection of haiku poetry. Yes, the mood and feeling in Reed's poems here are full-on autumn in both imagery and emotions.*
Written from obvious experiences in autumn landscapes, this is a terrific book. And the book blurb is

somewhat poetical too; that must be a first! The book is one to read again and again. As I will soon be doing!'
N.A.

'I really enjoyed reading this book of autumn haiku. Autumn is my favorite season, and I felt that Reed really captures the vibes and colors of autumn. The word choices were very intentional and powerful. I loved the sensory imagery.' L.V.

'It was such a pleasurable read.
Haiku is a special form of poetry, and P. J. Reed penned this collection of autumn haiku so beautifully. A beautiful read that I will recommend to all the haiku lovers.' K.

'A beautiful sensory collection of haiku that encapsulates Autumn in all its forms, with a fascinating insight into the author's inspiration.' B.R.

'St Andrew's Day, the last day of Autumn, an appropriate day to commend HAIKU GOLD, a captivating collection of seasonal Haiku that give a real flavour of recent days whether thinking about going out, being out walking, or back home relaxing and remembering the scenes experienced. The backstory of Haiku and glossary all add to the value of the volume.'
C.T.

Day	Haiku	No.
September		
22 September	a leaf floats slowly	21
23 September	feather discarded	22
24 September	blackberry petals	23
25 September	a patchwork of sky	24
26 September	after the night storm	25
27 September	swinging on the nuts	26
28 September	cow parsley statue	27
29 September	green leaves are drying	28
30 September	mushrooms have landed	29
October		
1 October	brown leaves wave farewell	33
2 October	clouds clutter the blue	34
3 October	sweet chestnut pompoms	35
4 October	fallen leaves wander	36
5 October	dragonfly flutters	37
6 October	evening brings the wind	38
7 October	dew soaked grass resprayed	39
8 October	amber everywhere	40
9 October	strung across the fence	41
10 October	fish play hide and seek	42
11 October	flotilla of ducks	43
12 October	hurricane spirits	44
13 October	forgotten grey path	45
14 October	windblown robin lands	46
15 October	shivering grasses	47
16 October	hidden fluffiness	48
17 October	rosehip aliens	49
18 October	heavy rain rattles	50
19 October	honking flap of geese	51
20 October	perched in my bird bowl	52
21 October	I walk on cloud tops	53

Haiku Gold

Haiku Gold: The Haiku Seasons Collection

SEPTEMBER

22 September

21

a leaf floats slowly
wandering with the river
autumn adventures

23 September

feather discarded
between paw prints and seashells
a seascape collage

24 September

23

blackberry petals
ripple while I watch and write
tempt me to their thorns

25 September

a patchwork of sky
greying clouds sewn together
with seams of sunlight

26 September

after the night storm
collage of ripped leaf and twig
lies beneath my feet

27 September

swinging on the nuts
squirrel dressed in brown and grey
rooks watch unamused

28 September

27

cow parsley statue
unleafed its crown is fading
life in sepia

29 September

green leaves are drying
fern fronds crackle under touch
trees are painted gold

30 September

29

mushrooms have landed
shiny saucers camouflaged
fungi in the fields

OCTOBER

1 October

33

brown leaves wave farewell
leap onto a gentle wind
the flight to freedom

2 October

34

clouds clutter the blue
watching as the lazing sun
falls from sleeping sky

3 October

35

sweet chestnut pompoms
balance on brown knotted twigs
spikes freshly sharpened

4 October

fallen leaves wander
taken by the lost canal
reflections ripple

5 October

37

dragonfly flutters
wings of finest cobweb silk
seen we walk away

6 October

evening brings the wind
strips flaming leaves from sad trees
night prefers the grey

7 October

39

dew soaked grass resprayed
blow dried by the sea blown wind
a green makeover

8 October

amber everywhere
russet hues on restless trees
grey clouds shaded red

9 October

41

strung across the fence
disappointment of pigeons
I bought the cheap seed

10 October

42

fish play hide and seek
bubbles burst on clear water
bulrush does not rush

11 October

43

flotilla of ducks
veer across the still water
a mallard mission

12 October

44

hurricane spirits
tossing twigs and plucking leaves
tries to steal my hat

13 October

45

forgotten grey path
clothed in golden autumn leaves
moments of beauty

14 October

46

windblown robin lands
feathers fluffed and breast polished
black rooks caw and rise

15 October

47

shivering grasses
the sun shines sideways shadows
sheep wander beneath

16 October

hidden fluffiness
four signets eat river grass
shielded by tree wall

17 October

49

rosehip aliens
bush full of red berry heads
star-mouthed and sightless

18 October

50

heavy rain rattles
swollen drops plop from grey trees
slowly a leaf falls

19 October

51

honking flap of geese
in varied 'v' formation
winter bags are packed

20 October

52

perched in my bird bowl
pigeon pecks its pumpkin seeds
birdhouse grows smaller

21 October

53

I walk on cloud tops
floating through the misted fields
the wind calls my name

22 October

54

bedazzled hawthorn
ruby covered prickled leaves
shimmy in the storm

23 October

55

blue periwinkles
glow through nettle underbush
sapphire stillness

24 October

56

morning sun stretches
gold leaves caught in sunlit rays
stayed for an instant

25 October

57

amber filtered trees
watch rook perched on chestnut top
crooks out his warning

26 October

58

mallard formations
acute angles on water
a quaking theorem

27 October

59

fungi in fatigues
tiny helmet trimmed with black
hidden in the grass

28 October

mossy lime feathers
drip from the stunted hedgerows
swaying in the breeze

29 October

61

silence of stilled trees
forest leaves left half-painted
nature unpeopled

30 October

62

distant orange haze
balloons bob in muddy fields
smells of Halloween

31 October

63

sycamore secrets
witches in dried seed bundles
watch from tattered twigs

Haiku Gold: The Haiku Seasons Collection

Haiku Gold: The Haiku Seasons Collection

NOVEMBER

Haiku Gold: The Haiku Seasons Collection

1 November

67

rodent rebranded
fancy black mouse in farmhouse
happy baby rat

2 November

68

pheasant feathers swirl
fluttering while fawn shadows
fly across the field

3 November

69

red berries no more
holly bush reduced to twigs
hungry wood pigeons

4 November

sly eastern winds blow
through the wavering grasses
betrayed by whispers

5 November

71

bonfires crackle
a haze of sulphur and ash
the night is on fire

6 November

72

loneliness of one
solitary leaf hanging
on an empty branch

7 November

73

empty chestnut trees
leaves shrink-wrapped and crumbling
conker shells to let

8 November

74

one touch of yellow
the birch leaves crumble and fall
I walk on crunches

9 November

75

the fields are hidden
curious clouds bent too low
falling from the sky

10 November

the last leaf showers
crash against crumbling soil
the trees are empty

11 November

77

the night leaned over
hid autumn trees in darkness
black leaves fall at night

12 November

stolen by the wind
unwrapped conker cases lie
prickling up the lane

13 November

79

fancy frilled layers
taupe toadstools in petticoats
dance in the downpour

14 November

evening never left
gull glides through grey metal sky
heavy raindrops fall

15 November

81

painting the field red
cherry leaves blaze amber flames
brambles turn to fire

16 November

curling and crunching
deep drifts of copper-blond leaves
lay across my path

17 November

83

the deep breath of fall
branches rattle as leaves chime
trees rock to the beat

18 November

84

Novembering days
cold rain splits the late sun rays
rainbows and storm clouds

19 November

85

untethered tree roots
trip and twirl across my path
hidden by leaf fall

20 November

86

the path is on fire
the amber leaves are dancing
autumn burns brightly

21 November

87

last of the leaf fall
an empty nest is revealed
ghost of chirpings past

22 November

days are darkening
grey trees stand silhouetted
against cloud drenched skies

23 November

89

tumbling golden leaves
play chase with the gusting wind
then fall at my feet

24 November

pole dancing nut thief
twisting round the bird feeder
wearing a fur coat

25 November

91

stubby grass whiskers
sprouting through the soggy mud
the fields are balding

26 November

92

gurgling stream giggles
white bubbles trapped in eddies
wash the river rocks

27 November

93

cherry tree in flames
ignited by silver moon
shadows turn and flee

28 November

storm clouds are stirring
salt sprayed mist climbs the valley
the sheep fields are paled

29 November

95

curious clouds pause
to watch themselves reflected
in crowded puddles

30 November

washed by salt sea spray
grasses blow dry in the wind
white waves curl and crash

DECEMBER

1 December

cold easterly wind
blows out the autumn colours
monochrome landscape

2 December

sunlight shines silver
filtered through nettled shadows
on rain watered paths

3 December

trees lost to shadow
half-moon hangs on greying sky
cloudless and alone

4 December

pine tree flaps and caws
rooks rise in their evening flight
the early dark fall

5 December

105

sun bleached and alone
abandoned by the storm swell
driftwood lays marooned

6 December

ridden by the wind
foaming waves race and gallop
headland lost in mist

7 December

evening has fallen
dew sprinkled bushes sparkle
the left leaves shiver

8 December

heavy rain bounces
walking in a fallen cloud
wellies start to sink

9 December

untamed and jiggling
the stinging nettles wobble
rain rinsed and polished

10 December

windswept clouds painted
in swirls of sunlit silver
drip into the fields

11 December

days of the dark fall
the world is draped in shadows
winter is coming

12 December

112

morning after storm
graveyard of seashells and stone
beneath clear waters

13 December

113

winter is stirring
plucks leaves from the frowning trees
covers browning lane

14 December

114

snow filled clouds gather
tumble across silver sky
the first snowflakes fall

15 December

115

covered in cracked ice
unreflecting clouds and sky
the pond lies silent

16 December

days are darkening
grey trees stand silhouetted
against cloud drenched skies

17 December

117

icy solitude
fields painted in monochrome
silence of snowfall

18 December

the empty oak tree
roots reflected in the clouds
sleep beneath the frost

19 December

119

mistletoe kisses
balls of leaves on empty trees
decorating Yule

20 December

inside the snow globe
frost covered branches shiver
silent snowflakes fall

21 December

laughing steeple bells
strike through the misted valley
strength of centuries

Haiku Ice

To continue your daily haiku journey through the changing seasons, step into 'Haiku Ice.'

Winter is a season of frozen beauty and the slowing of time, as a white breath falls against the browning leaves and winter tightens its grip over the sleeping landscape. It is a time of solitude and reflection as people and animals shelter from the cold as a frozen quietness settles on the countryside.

'This enchanting collection will keep you company for every day of winter. Pictures of winter recorded as haiku for everyone to experience and enjoy.'

'Haiku Ice' is available from Amazon and all good bookshops.

https://www.amazon.co.uk/dp/B07R1LL1RQ

Appendix One

How to Write Haiku

Everyone has his or her own writing style, and it is always important to let your writer's voice come through in your writing. Some forms of poetry are defined by their structure: two-line Urdu love poetry; sonnets, which are fourteen-line poems written in iambic pentameter; and limericks, which use a five-line anapaestic metre and a strict AABBA rhyme scheme.

Writing a traditional *haiku* is an exercise in bending your words into a concise structure. Many poets liken the art of *haiku* writing to playing chess: it requires strategy and mathematical precision. As with any skill, *haiku* needs practice, and with practice you develop a way of thinking that automatically responds to the 5-7-5 syllable scheme that is immediately recognised throughout the world as *haiku*.

A traditional *haiku* contains three lines: the first and last with five *morae*, the middle with seven. A *mora* is a unit of sound in Japanese. It is similar to a syllable in English, though not equivalent. Since *morae* cannot be directly translated, Western adaptations use syllables instead. An English *haiku* typically follows a 5–7–5 syllable pattern across three lines.

Traditional *haiku* have no title, no rhyme, and usually no punctuation. However, they often include a *kireji,* a verbal punctuation, and a *kigo,* which is a seasonal reference.

A *haiku* usually presents a juxtaposition in the first or third line, dividing the poem into contrasting parts. Nature and the seasons are central themes, with thoughts and feelings distilled into a single breath.

I find my best writing moments are away from people, just walking with my dog or alone and watching nature without the hindrance of man. I have often been asked by the few passers-by what I was doing, as I stood and memorised the mechanics of a droplet of water falling from a leaf.

On these occasions, it is always better to reply that you are writing *haiku* and not, in fact, watching a leaf. One reply will get responses such as 'very noble' and 'how exciting!'. The other will get you a sideways glance and a wide berth.

Once I have observed and the tingling of a *haiku* begins to form, I try to write down, normally in the first two lines, what I have just seen.

The juxtaposition comes in the final line and will be either a comment on the picture formed, an extension of the image to other areas, the picture from a differing point of view, or even what happened afterwards. So, while the last line is still related to the first, it is obviously different.

One way I teach my students to write *haiku* is by encouraging them to truly observe nature through their senses.

It's what I call *'Investigating the Leaf.'*

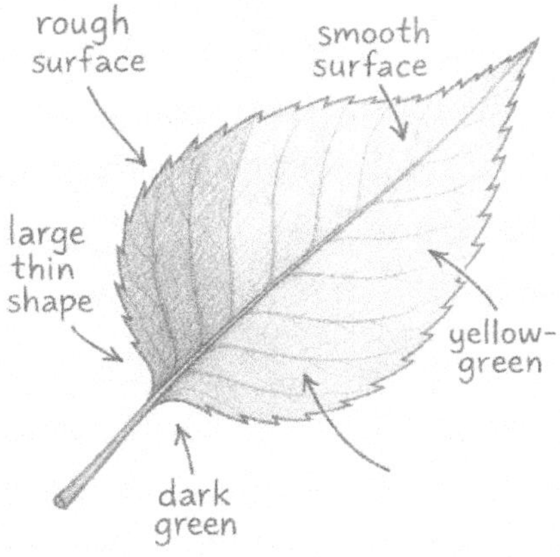

1. Go outside and pick up the first leaf you find on the ground in front of you. Bring it inside and sketch it.
2. Annotate the leaf by carefully observing its qualities and answering these questions:

> Is the surface rough or smooth?
> What do the edges look like thin or thick, even or jagged?
> Is it big or small?
> Can you describe and label the different colours of the leaf?
> What do you imagine the leaf saw as it fell?
> How do the tree and/or leaf feel?
> What did it feel like when it landed?

3. You should now have a leaf sketch filled with beautiful observations. Write each description on a

separate line. So, you have between five and ten lines of emotive, descriptive prose poetry.

4. Pick your two favourite lines and rewrite them so that the first line has five syllables, and the second has seven.

5. For the third and final line, choose one of your emotive phrases something that captures how the leaf or tree *feels* and rewrite it as five syllables.

6. Finally, put the three completed lines together, and there you are! Congratulations! You've written a haiku! Hopefully, the first of many.

Appendix Two

A Brief History of Haiku

Haiku is an ancient Japanese poetic art form whose roots stretch back to the Heian period (794–1185), a golden age of Japanese culture and refinement. During this era, poetry was not merely a pastime but an essential marker of education, taste, and social grace. Members of the court and literati were expected to recognise, compose, and participate in *renga,* a collaborative form of linked-verse poetry performed at elegant gatherings and lavish salons.

Renga was among the most esteemed literary arts of pre-modern Japan. It was composed according to alternating patterns of 5–7–5 and 7–7 sound units, often continuing for dozens or even hundreds of stanzas. Each poet would contribute a verse, weaving together a shared tapestry of imagery, mood, and seasonal reference. The poem's final stanzas, typically written in the 7–7 rhythm, provided a graceful closure to this collective act of creation.

Central to the *renga* tradition was the pursuit of *utakotoba,* refined poetic diction that elevated ordinary language into an art form. The use of colloquial or unpolished phrasing was considered unsuitable for serious verse; elegance and restraint defined true poetry.

The opening verse of a *renga* sequence was called the *hokku,* and it held a position of special honour. Often composed by the host or a distinguished guest, the *hokku* established the mood, setting, and season of the entire poem. Structurally, it consisted of seventeen *morae* (sound units), arranged in three phrases of 5, 7, and 5. Unlike Western syllables, *morae* reflect rhythm and timing rather than pronunciation length, giving the verse its distinct cadence. The *hokku* also contained a *kireji*, or 'cutting word,' which served as a pause or point of emphasis, lending the poem emotional or tonal depth. Traditionally, *hokku* were written vertically from top to bottom in elegant brush calligraphy.

In the sixteenth century, during a time of social upheaval and the rise of the Tokugawa shogunate, Japanese poetry began to evolve. The rigid formality of courtly *waka* gave way to more spontaneous, accessible verse. It was within this shifting landscape that the grand *haiku* master Matsuo Bashō (1644–1694) transformed the *hokku* into an independent art form. Bashō elevated it beyond its ceremonial function, using it to capture transient moments of beauty, melancholy, and insight, which he called *sabi* (lonely elegance) and *wabi* (humble simplicity).

By Bashō's time, the *hokku* could appear alone or be paired with prose in *haibun*, or with paintings in *haiga*. These hybrid forms reflected the Japanese ideal of unity between word, image, and spirit.

In the late nineteenth century, the modern poet Masaoka Shiki (1867–1902) gave this evolved form its contemporary name - *haiku*. Through his efforts to modernise and simplify Japanese poetry, Shiki redefined the *hokku* as a self-contained poem, brief yet profound, grounded in observation, and alive with seasonal awareness.

Haiku first reached the Western world in the late nineteenth century, during a period of growing cultural exchange between Japan and Europe. Following Japan's Meiji Restoration in 1868, the country opened its borders after centuries of isolation. Scholars, diplomats, and travelers began to encounter the concise, image-driven beauty of Japanese poetry and brought it back to their own literary circles.

Early Western readers discovered haiku through translation. The first English renderings appeared in the 1890s, often produced by missionaries, linguists, and academics who admired the simplicity and precision of the form. Among these early voices were Basil Hall Chamberlain, a British scholar who published translations of classical Japanese poems, and Lafcadio Hearn, whose writings introduced Japanese art and folklore to Western audiences.

However, it was not until the early twentieth century that *haiku* truly took root in Western literature. Ezra Pound and other Imagist poets found in *haiku* an ideal model for clarity and economy of language. They were drawn to its focus on the concrete moment, the absence of ornament, and its capacity to suggest vast emotion in a few short lines.

Pound's poem 'In a Station of the Metro,' was directly inspired by Japanese verse, and its influence marked a turning point in modernist poetry.

Throughout the twentieth century, *haiku* spread rapidly across Europe and America. Writers such as R. H. Blyth played a crucial role in this movement. Blyth's four-volume series 'Haiku' (1949–1952) presented Japanese masters like Bashō, Buson, and Issa to an English-speaking audience with insightful commentary. His books were later read by poets of the Beat Generation, including Jack Kerouac and Gary Snyder, who embraced *haiku* as a form of spontaneous, Zen-influenced expression.

By the 1960s, *haiku* had become a recognised part of Western poetic practice. Literary journals, anthologies, and societies dedicated to English-language *haiku* began to appear, particularly in the United States and the United Kingdom.

Today, *haiku* thrives as a global art form. It is written in dozens of languages and practiced by poets from every background. Though transformed by translation and adaptation, its essence endures: a brief, vivid encounter with the living world, where silence speaks as powerfully as words.

Appendix Three

137

The Haiku Glossary

Aika	An elegy. A poem of serious reflection, usually a lament for the dead.
Engo	A word association. A kind of poetic echo that links words by shared meaning, mood, or cultural resonance, such as 'rain / reflection / memory.'
Fuga	Means something closer to 'elegant taste' or 'refined beauty.' It appears in classical poetry and art criticism: the sense of grace, subtlety, and cultured restraint. A *haiku* described as *fuga* will contain quiet sophistication, harmony, and emotional precision rather than drama.
Fukinsei	Celebrating the beauty of asymmetry, irregularity, and the imbalance of nature, finding harmony in the irregular, uneven, and imperfect.
Fūryū	*Fūryū* means 'refined elegance touched by the fleeting.' It literally translates to 'wind and flow,' which already tells you something: grace that moves, beauty in motion, sophistication that's natural rather than stiff.
	Fūryū isn't about polish; it's about effortless taste. A moment so vivid or balanced that it feels both spontaneous and artful.

Gojuin	*A fifty-link renga.*
Ginko	A walk taken with the specific purpose of observing nature to find inspiration for writing haiku. This is what I call my 'Haiku Safaris.'
Haibun	A combination of prose and *haiku*. The prose part of the *haibun* often describes a scene or a moment, sometimes in a travel diary or autobiographical style. The *haiku,* placed at the end or interspersed, serves to deepen the meaning or add a new layer of insight to the prose.
Haiga	A picture combined with *haiku*.
Haigon	When a *haiku* is written in the language of common people using vulgar or plain speech or everyday images, such as 'mud on my sandals.'
Haijin	The writer of *haiku*.
Haiku	*Haiku* is a highly structured form of Japanese poetry. In Western culture, haiku is easily recognisable from micro-poetry by its structure. *Haiku* consists of three lines. The first line contains five syllables, the second seven syllables and the third five syllables. Traditional *haiku* must contain certain elements, such as a *kigo* and a seasonal element. It consists of a moment in nature captured and recorded.

Haiku Moment	The intense focus on one moment in time. To capture and freeze that image in *haiku* before it is lost or altered by the passage of time.
Hokku	The original form of *haiku*. The opening stanza of a *renga*. A long poem written by many people as a form of entertainment for the ruling elite of Japanese society.
Juxtaposition	When sentences are placed together with a contrasting or 'cutting' effect. It is the first or third line of the *haiku*.
Kigo	A word that implies the season of the haiku.
Kireji	A cutting word that denotes a break between the two parts of the *haiku* when writing in one-line Japanese poetry. There is no English equivalent of this, although some poets may put a dash in their *haiku* to denote the change.
Koan	A *koan* is a Zen Buddhist contemplative phrase that contains a logical contradiction or paradox designed to challenge the reader
Mora	The *mora* is a unit of sound in the Japanese language, which is like a syllable, but not the same.
Sabi	The innate loneliness of life, perhaps something old and faded. It is a reminder of the impermanence of life.

Senryu	A form of human *haiku*, expressing emotions or human actions. It has the same structure as *haiku* but does not have to contain a cutting word.
Syllable	A syllable is a single sound unit of a word.
Tanka	A *tanka* is similar to haiku but consists of five lines and thirty-one syllables. Each line has a set number of syllables; see below.

Line one–five syllables
Line two–seven syllables
Line three–five syllables
Line four–seven syllables
Line five–seven syllables

Utamakura	'Pillow Words' used to evoke specific associations.
Wabi	The austere and severe beauty of nature expressed through writings of spiritual solitude.
Waka	Traditional Japanese poetry.
Yojo	*Yojo* is the way of using words that goes beyond their superficial meaning. The words of the *haiku* have a deeper, more spiritual or emotional meaning.
Zoku	A creative force of nature that is expressed through seasonal transformation.

www.ingramcontent.com/pod-product-compliance
Lightning Source LLC
Chambersburg PA
CBHW060937050726
47592CB00003B/1001